Computer Store

By Jennifer Colby

21st Century **Junior** Library

Published in the United States of America by
Cherry Lake Publishing
Ann Arbor, Michigan
www.cherrylakepublishing.com

Content Adviser: Keith Voelker, Network Engineer
Reading Adviser: Marla Conn MS, Ed., Literacy specialist, Read-Ability, Inc.

Photo Credits: © goodluz/Shutterstock Images, cover, 1; ©dotshock/Shutterstock Images, 4; © Diego Cervo/Shutterstock Images, 6; ©warrengoldswain/Shutterstock Images, 8; © kadmy/Shutterstock Images, 10; © Korta/Shutterstock Images, 12; © jordanfotografi/Shutterstock Images, 14; © jmalov/iStock Images, 16; © Monkey Business Images/Shutterstock Images, 18; © Andor Bujdoso/Shutterstock Images, 20

Library of Congress Cataloging-in-Publication Data
Names: Colby, Jennifer, 1971- author.
Title: Computer store / by Jennifer Colby.
Description: Ann Arbor : Cherry Lake Publishing, [2016] | Series: 21st century junior library. Explore a workplace | Audience: K to grade 3.
Identifiers: LCCN 2015047470| ISBN 9781634710787 (hardcover) | ISBN 9781634712767 (pbk.) | ISBN 9781634711777 (pdf) | ISBN 9781634713757 (ebook)
Subjects: LCSH: Computer stores—Juvenile literature. | Technology—Vocational guidance—Juvenile literature.
Classification: LCC HD9696.2.A2 C64 2016 | DDC 381.45004023—dc23
LC record available at http://lccn.loc.gov/2015047470

Cherry Lake Publishing would like to acknowledge the work of The Partnership for 21st Century Learning. Please visit *www.p21.org* for more information.

Printed in the United States of America
Corporate Graphics

CONTENTS

You can shop for a computer at a computer store.

What Is a Computer Store?

Look at the computers all around you. Some have big screens. Some are so small you can carry them with you. There are computers of all shapes and sizes. Where are you? You are at a computer store!

Computer store workers help you find what you are looking for.

Some people go to the computer store to buy a computer or computer parts. Some go to learn how to use a computer. Others need to get their computers fixed by a **technician**.

Computer store workers can help you in many ways. Each worker has a different job to do. Would you like to work at a computer store? Let's learn about computer store workers.

Look!

Look around the computer store. You might see things besides computers. What else is sold there? Phones and **printers** may also be sold there.

Store managers meet with people who are looking for jobs.

Computer Store Workers

Most stores have multiple **managers**. One manager is in charge of the **salespeople**. Another manager is in charge of the technicians. Another manager hires the people who work at the store. This manager decides if a person would make a good computer store worker.

A salesperson can tell you about new computers and special sales.

Managers talk with workers. They also like to talk with **customers**. They like to hear what you think. They want to make the store run better.

Who else has a job at a computer store? Salespeople answer your questions. They tell you about what is sold in the store. They help you decide which computer is right for you.

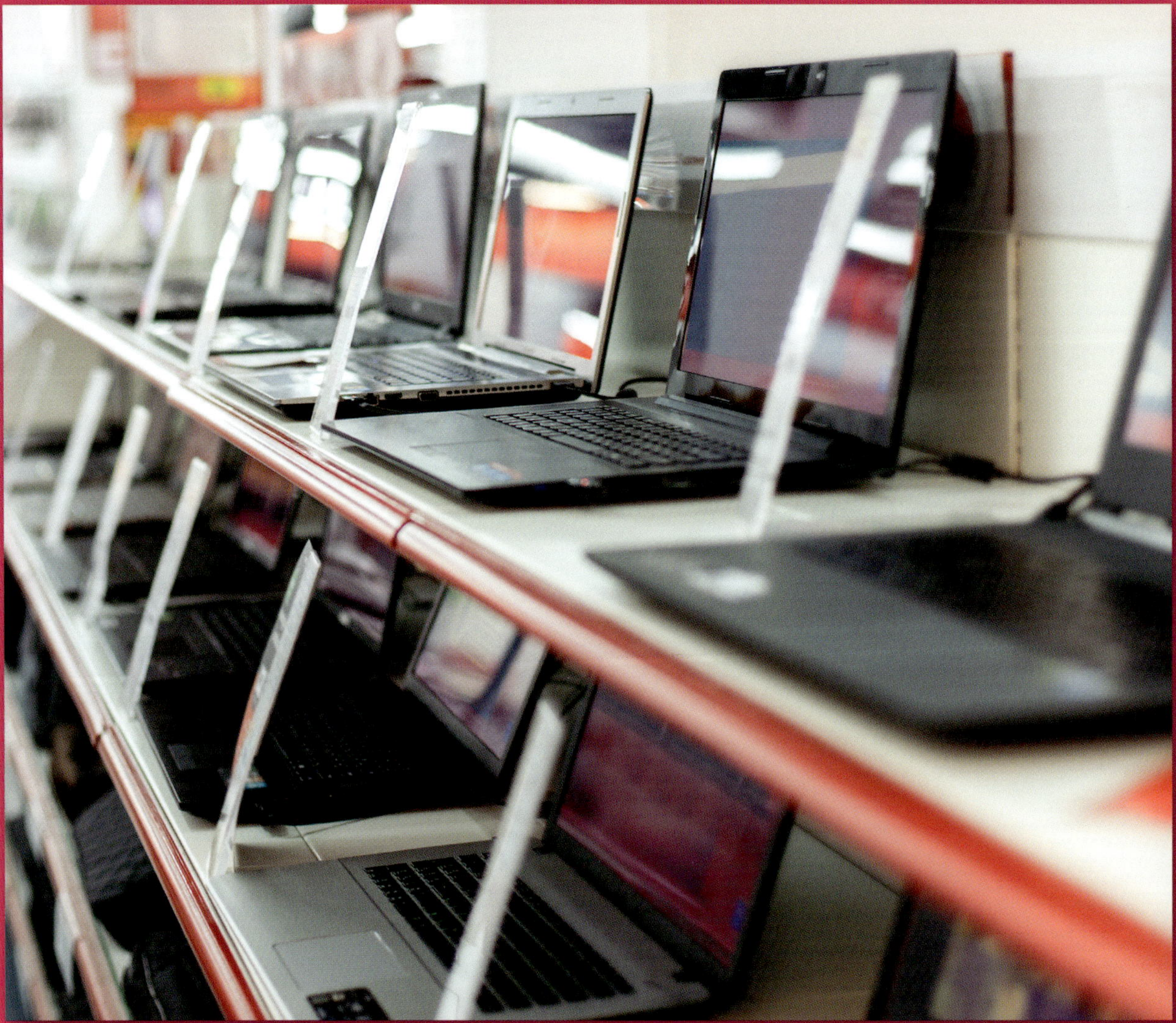

There are many items to choose from in a computer store.

Computer stores sell many different things. The store has different sections. Salespeople know about the products in each section. They help you find what you need.

A technician may need to take apart your computer to find out why it isn't working.

Who can help you if your computer does not work? Most computer stores have technicians. A store technician can talk with you to find out what is wrong. The technician can fix your computer if it is broken.

Make a Guess!

Guess how many types of computers are in a store. Remember that the technician needs to know how to fix each one. Look for the technician when you are at a computer store. Ask if your guess was correct.

You need to pay for your computer before you can take it home.

Do you like your new computer? Maybe not. You want to **return** it. Talk to a customer service worker. That person will help you.

Do you see why a computer store needs many workers? They all want to help you find and use the computer that is right for you!

Do you like computers? Maybe you should work at a computer store!

Do You Want to Work at a Computer Store?

If you want to work in a computer store, learn as much as you can about computers. Try using different kinds of computers at your school or public library. Practice talking about computers with your friends and family.

Ask Questions!

Do you want a job at a computer store? Talk to workers when you visit. Ask them about their jobs. What do they do? What do they like best? Their answers can help you decide.

Someday, you could show computer store customers how to use their computers.

The next time you visit a computer store think about your favorite part of the experience. Is it talking to a salesperson? Or maybe getting advice from a technician? There are many different jobs to choose from in a computer store. Maybe one of those jobs is right for you!

GLOSSARY

customers (KUHS-tuh-murz) people who buy items or pay for a service

managers (MAN-uh-jurz) people who are in charge

printers (PRINT-urz) machines that can print information from a computer

return (ri-TURN) to bring something you bought back to the place that it came from

salespeople (SAYLZ-pee-puhl) workers who help you decide what to buy

technicians (tek-NISH-uhnz) workers who fix broken computers

FIND OUT MORE

BOOKS

Cunningham, Kevin. *Computers*. Ann Arbor: Cherry Lake Publishing, 2009.

Zuchora-Walske, Christine. *What's Inside My Computer?* Minneapolis: Lerner Publications, 2015.

WEB SITES

Code.org—Learn an Hour of Code
https://code.org/learn
Try a fun and interactive computer programming activity.

Your Dictionary—Computer Terms for Children
http://grammar.yourdictionary.com/word-lists/computer-terms-for-children.html
Learn computer vocabulary terms to better understand how to work with computers.

INDEX

ABOUT THE AUTHOR

Jennifer Colby is the author of many books for children. She is a high school librarian in Michigan. She enjoys teaching her students how to use computers. Her first computer as a child was an Apple IIe.